The road to Palestine

Dans Hardyans

Foreword

"The Road to Palestine" is not a path for the faint-hearted. It is a journey forged by sacrifice, resilience, and an unyielding hope for justice. Palestine, a land revered by many, stands as a symbol of human endurance against oppression and adversity.

This book is not meant to point fingers or ignite divisions. Instead, it seeks to illuminate the truth—that Palestine is a victim of a conflict it did not choose. The stories within these pages reflect the courage of a people who have been denied their basic rights but continue to rise, even in the face of overwhelming odds.

Through history, narratives of survival, and personal accounts, this book aims to shed light on the plight of the Palestinian people. It is a call to the world to not look away but to empathize and act in the spirit of humanity and justice.

Welcome to the journey—may it open your eyes and stir your soul.

—

#1 A Land Caught in Conflict

The Cradle of Civilizations

Palestine, a land mentioned in sacred texts and cherished by three major religions, has always been a meeting point of cultures and faiths. For centuries, it was a place where Jews, Christians, and Muslims coexisted in relative harmony, their lives intertwined in a shared reverence for the land.

But this harmony was shattered in the early 20th century when geopolitical ambitions and colonial interests began to unravel the fabric of coexistence. The Balfour Declaration of 1917 marked the beginning of Palestine's struggle, as foreign powers carved out territories and displaced native populations.

By 1948, the establishment of the state of Israel brought about the Nakba—or "catastrophe"—when hundreds of thousands of Palestinians were uprooted from their homes, their towns destroyed, and their rights dismissed. What followed was decades of occupation, blockades, and an enduring struggle for self-determination.

A People Dispossessed

To be Palestinian today is to carry the weight of history and the scars of displacement. For those living under occupation, daily life is a series of struggles: passing through checkpoints, living in homes under constant threat of demolition, and facing restrictions that hinder even the most basic freedoms.

For those in exile, it is a longing for a home they may never see again. Refugee camps across neighboring countries are filled with generations of Palestinians who dream of returning to their ancestral lands, even as the years turn into decades.

The Global Silence

Perhaps the most painful aspect of Palestine's story is the silence of the world. While international laws are violated, and human rights are disregarded, the global response often wavers between apathy and indifference. This silence, deliberate or otherwise, only deepens the suffering of the Palestinian people.

A Symbol of Resistance

Yet, despite it all, Palestine endures. It stands not just as a geographical location but as a symbol of resistance against oppression. From the olive trees that are replanted after being uprooted to the children who continue their education under the shadow of destruction, the spirit of Palestine remains unbroken.

Reflection

This chapter serves as a reminder that the road to Palestine is paved with pain, perseverance, and an unwavering hope for justice. As you turn these pages, let the stories of this land and its people inspire you to see beyond headlines and statistics. This is not just their struggle—it is a call for all of humanity to stand on the side of justice and compassion.

#2 The Struggle Within the Shadows

Under the Weight of Blockades

Life in Gaza is defined by boundaries—physical, economic, and emotional. The blockade, a seemingly endless siege, has turned this strip of land into one of the most densely populated and impoverished areas in the world. Basic necessities, such as clean water, electricity, and medical supplies, are scarce, leaving millions in a state of perpetual crisis.

The blockade is not just a barrier; it is a daily reminder of isolation. Hospitals operate without essential equipment. Fishermen are restricted to waters too shallow to yield a meaningful catch. Students dream of education abroad but are denied the chance to leave. Yet, amidst these challenges, the people of Gaza find ways to adapt, resist, and survive.

Stories of Survival

Fatima, a mother of four, wakes up every day at dawn to bake bread for her children. Her husband was killed during one of the conflicts, leaving her to fend for the family. "The hardest part," she says, "is not knowing if we'll have food tomorrow." Yet, her strength is unyielding. She teaches her children to write, to read, to hope.

Her eldest son, Ahmed, dreams of becoming a doctor. "I want to help my people," he says. But the lack of opportunities and constant interruptions to schooling make this dream feel like a distant star.

The Spirit of Resistance

Despite the challenges, Gaza is alive with resilience. Artists paint murals on walls scarred by bombings. Musicians compose songs of hope and longing. Teachers, often unpaid, continue to educate, knowing that knowledge is a powerful weapon against oppression.

What the World Doesn't See

The mainstream narrative often reduces Gaza to a conflict zone, overlooking the humanity of its people. Fatima's laughter as she plays with her children, Ahmed's determination to study under candlelight, and the communal spirit that binds neighborhoods together—these are stories that rarely make headlines but are the essence of Gaza's strength.

A Call for Justice

The blockade is not merely a physical barrier; it is a symbol of the global community's failure to uphold human rights. But it is also a testament to the unyielding spirit of a people who refuse to be forgotten.

#3 A Home Behind Walls

Life at the Checkpoints

In the West Bank, the rhythm of life is dictated by checkpoints. Every journey—whether to school, work, or the market—is interrupted by the looming presence of barriers manned by armed guards. For Palestinians, crossing these checkpoints is a daily ordeal, an exercise in patience and survival.

A young man named Ibrahim works as a teacher in a village near Ramallah. His commute, which should take twenty minutes, often stretches into hours due to delays at the checkpoints. "They don't tell us why we wait," he says. "We just stand there, hoping they'll let us pass." The uncertainty eats away at time, energy, and dignity, but Ibrahim persists. "Education is our resistance," he adds.

A Landscape Divided

Beyond the checkpoints, walls snake through the West Bank, dividing towns, cutting off farmers from their land, and encroaching on Palestinian territories. These walls, often adorned with graffiti expressing anger and hope, are physical reminders of separation and dispossession.

For Amal, an elderly woman, the wall stands where her family's olive grove once flourished. "My father planted those trees," she says, her voice tinged with grief. "Now, I can only see them from a distance." Her loss is shared by countless others who watch their heritage and livelihood slip away.

The Fragility of Normalcy

Despite the walls, checkpoints, and restrictions, life in the West Bank goes on. Markets buzz with activity, children play soccer in alleys, and weddings are celebrated with joyful defiance. This semblance of normalcy is a quiet form of resistance—a refusal to let oppression extinguish the spirit of community.

International Silence and Complicity

While the world often debates the politics of the region, the human cost remains overlooked. The restrictions, the walls, and the erasure of Palestinian identity are violations of international law, yet the global response remains tepid. The silence is deafening, and its impact is felt most by those who live behind these barriers.

Reflections on Injustice

The walls may divide the land, but they cannot erase the resilience of its people. Ibrahim's determination to teach, Amal's memories of her olive grove, and the enduring hope of millions are testaments to a spirit that refuses to be broken.

#4 Children of Conflict

Born Into Struggle

For many Palestinian children, the concept of a carefree childhood is almost non-existent. They are born into a reality where the sounds of laughter often mix with the echoes of gunfire, and dreams of the future are shadowed by the uncertainty of survival.

Amina, an eight-year-old from Khan Younis in Gaza, speaks with wisdom far beyond her years. "When I grow up, I want to be a journalist," she says. "I want the world to know what happens to us." Her words reflect a painful truth: Palestinian children are witnesses to a conflict that forces them to mature too quickly.

The Classroom as a Battleground

Education is a fundamental right, but in occupied Palestine, it is a battleground. Schools are frequently disrupted by raids, closures, and bombings. Teachers persevere despite inadequate resources, overcrowded classrooms, and the ever-present threat of violence.

In Hebron, a teacher named Rami walks through hostile checkpoints daily to reach his students. "They deserve a chance to learn," he says. His classroom, a modest room with peeling paint and mismatched desks, is a sanctuary of hope. "Education is how we fight back," he adds.

Lost Innocence

Playgrounds in Palestine often carry an air of tension. Children play soccer amidst rubble, their laughter punctuated by distant explosions. For many, toys are a luxury, and their games are shaped by their surroundings.

A group of boys in a refugee camp recreate scenes they've witnessed, using sticks as rifles and stones as their defense. While their innocence shines through, their games are a stark reminder of the realities they face.

Trauma and Resilience

The psychological scars of conflict are profound. Nightmares, anxiety, and a pervasive sense of insecurity plague many Palestinian children. Yet, there is also resilience. They draw strength from their families, communities, and their shared determination to endure.

Amina, who dreams of being a journalist, captures this resilience in her notebook filled with drawings and stories. "This is my way of being brave," she says. "When I feel scared, I write."

The World's Responsibility

Children are the most vulnerable victims of any conflict, and Palestinian children are no exception. Their plight demands not pity, but action. It is the responsibility of the global community to ensure that these children have a chance to dream, to learn, and to live without fear.

Hope Amidst the Chaos

Despite the hardships, Palestinian children continue to hope. Their laughter, creativity, and unbreakable spirit are reminders that even in the darkest times, the human spirit can shine brightly.

#5 The Olive Tree and the Land of Generations

Roots in the Soil

The olive tree is not just a symbol of peace; for Palestinians, it is the embodiment of their connection to the land. Planted by their ancestors, these trees have witnessed the ebb and flow of time, standing firm through wars, invasions, and occupations.

But for many Palestinians, the olive tree represents something far more personal: it is a link to family, to memory, and to a heritage that is being gradually erased. The land that holds these trees is the same land their forefathers tended to, the same land their children long to return to.

The Struggle for Land

Land confiscation, settlement expansion, and the ever-growing network of Israeli-controlled areas make it nearly impossible for Palestinians to freely cultivate their land. Farmers are often harassed, their crops destroyed, and their olive trees uprooted. But despite the hardships, the olive tree continues to grow, its roots entrenched deep in the soil, much like the spirit of the Palestinian people.

Youssef, a farmer from the West Bank, recalls the day Israeli settlers arrived to destroy his olive grove. "They came with bulldozers," he says. "They didn't care that these trees were planted by my grandfather." The loss was devastating, but Youssef didn't give up. He replanted his trees, knowing that each olive branch would bear witness to his persistence. "This land is ours," he declares. "Even if they take our trees, we will keep planting."

A Symbol of Defiance

The olive tree is often seen as a symbol of peace, but in Palestine, it is also a symbol of resistance. When the Israeli military attempted to uproot olive trees as a method of punishment, Palestinians would replant them, defying the occupation and asserting their right to the land.

In the village of Beit Jala, residents rallied together after a series of tree uprootings. "We gathered as a community and replanted," recalls Fatima, a local activist. "The trees are not just for us; they are for our children, and for their children. They are a symbol of our persistence."

Loss and Hope

Losing a tree is not just about losing a piece of land; it's about losing a connection to one's heritage and future. Every uprooted olive tree carries with it a memory, a story, and a sense of belonging. Yet, the Palestinian spirit refuses to let these losses define them. In the face of destruction, the act of planting a new tree becomes an act of resilience, a statement that no matter how many trees are lost, they will continue to grow.

The Global Response

While the olive tree represents hope and strength for Palestinians, the international community's response to the destruction of these symbols is often muted. The world's silence in the face of these violations is a reminder of the ongoing struggles for justice that Palestinians continue to endure.

However, as more and more individuals around the world stand in solidarity with Palestine, the act of planting olive trees in support of Palestinian farmers has become a powerful symbol of global resistance. Organizations and individuals worldwide are recognizing the importance of these trees, both as a symbol of Palestinian heritage and as a form of resistance to occupation.

Reflections on Legacy

The olive tree, deeply rooted in the soil, continues to thrive despite the odds. It is a symbol of the land's deep connection to the Palestinian people, one that no force can easily sever. Even as olive groves are destroyed, the act of replanting speaks of a future where the spirit of the land, and its people, endures.

#6 The Weight of Silence: The World's Inaction

A Call for Justice Ignored

For decades, the cries of the Palestinian people have echoed through the corridors of international institutions, yet they often fall on deaf ears. The United Nations, human rights organizations, and governments worldwide have condemned the violence, the occupation, and the displacement, but little tangible action has followed.

This silence speaks volumes, not only about the situation in Palestine but about the broader failure of the global community to uphold justice and human rights. Palestinians are left wondering: Why does the world continue to turn a blind eye to their suffering?

International Complicity

Behind the silence lies a complex web of geopolitical interests. Countries with strong ties to Israel often find themselves caught in a delicate balancing act, choosing diplomacy over action, political alliance over humanitarian concerns. This has led to a situation where the violation of Palestinian rights has become almost normalized, treated as an inevitable consequence of the conflict rather than a breach of international law.

In Ramallah, Sami, a lawyer who has spent his life advocating for Palestinian rights, speaks about the frustration of international indifference: "When we call for accountability, we are met with political excuses. People who suffer because of this silence don't care about politics—they care about justice."

The Role of the Media

Media coverage of the Palestinian-Israeli conflict is often skewed or one-sided. Western media outlets tend to focus on the violence that erupts between the two sides, framing the issue as a "two-sided conflict" rather than addressing the systemic injustices Palestinians face daily.

This portrayal not only misrepresents the realities on the ground but also perpetuates the narrative that Palestinians are complicit in their own suffering. Through selective reporting, the media has contributed to the erasure of Palestinian voices, leaving many unaware of the true nature of the occupation.

The Struggle for Recognition

While international organizations often issue statements calling for peace and negotiations, they rarely hold the powerful accountable for their actions. Palestinians, it seems, are forever caught in a cycle of promises and empty gestures, with little to show for their years of suffering.

Zainab, a mother who lost her home in a demolition, reflects on the lack of recognition for their struggle: "They talk about peace, but where is the justice? No one has come to fix what has been broken here. The world speaks of peace but forgets the pain."

The Power of Solidarity

Though the international community's response remains sluggish, grassroots movements and activists around the world continue to raise their voices in solidarity with the Palestinian cause. These movements, though not always supported by governments, represent a growing awareness that the Palestinian struggle for freedom and justice is a human issue, not just a political one.

From organizing protests to pushing for divestment from companies that profit from the occupation, these movements are making it clear that the Palestinian cause is not just a regional issue but a global one. In cities across the world, people are demanding accountability, justice, and an end to the oppression of Palestinians.

The Weight of Hope

Even in the face of international indifference, the Palestinian people continue to hope. They continue to struggle, to resist, and to speak their truth. Their cries for justice may be met with silence, but their will to persist will never be silenced.

The world may remain indifferent, but as long as there are people willing to listen, there is hope. The fight for justice is long, but it is a fight that must continue—because the cost of silence is too great.

#7 The Power of Resilience: Life Under Occupation

Endurance Through Adversity

For Palestinians, resilience is not a choice—it is a necessity. It is woven into every aspect of daily life, from the determination to survive each day under the constant threat of violence, to the persistence in holding on to their cultural identity, even when every effort is made to strip it away.

In the city of Nablus, a young woman named Layla opens her small shop in the early hours of the morning. She sells handmade embroidery, a craft passed down through generations of Palestinian women. "This work reminds me of my grandmother," Layla says, her hands gently placing a finished piece on display. "It is more than just art—it is a statement that we are still here."

Life in the Shadow of the Wall

The separation wall, a physical manifestation of the occupation, cuts through Palestinian communities, isolating families, restricting movement, and preventing access to vital resources. But the wall, while an instrument of division, has also become a symbol of resilience. Palestinians living on either side of the wall continue to defy its purpose, refusing to be silenced by its concrete barriers.

In Bethlehem, a city divided by the wall, Ahmed, a teacher, takes his students on a walk along the barrier. "This is not just a wall," he says. "It is a challenge. It tells us that they want us to be separated, to forget who we are. But look at the art that covers it—look at how we use it to tell our stories." The wall, now covered in murals and graffiti, stands not as a barrier, but as a canvas for Palestinian voices.

The Palestinian Spirit: Unbreakable, Unyielding

Every act of resistance, no matter how small, is a testament to the unyielding spirit of the Palestinian people. From mothers who continue to bake bread and teach their children despite curfews and checkpoints, to farmers who risk their lives to tend their land, resilience is everywhere.

In Gaza, where life is marked by the scarcity of resources and constant bombardment, a group of young activists have organized community gardens to grow food. "We can't wait for the world to help us," says Amira, one of the organizers. "We have to take action, even in the darkest times." These gardens, symbols of self-reliance and defiance, provide food and hope for families who have seen their homes reduced to rubble.

Art as Resistance

Palestinian artists have long used their craft as a tool for resistance, a way to reclaim their narrative in the face of occupation. Through music, poetry, theater, and visual art, they give voice to the struggles of their people, drawing attention to the ongoing injustice.

At an underground art gallery in Ramallah, a collection of paintings, photographs, and sculptures tell the story of Palestine's pain, beauty, and hope. "Art is a way to remind the world that we are still here," says Zaid, an artist whose work depicts scenes of daily life in Palestine. "It is how we resist without using violence."

A Legacy of Resilience

The resilience of the Palestinian people is not just a present-day phenomenon; it is a legacy passed down through generations. It is a resilience born of struggle, but also of hope. For the older generation, it is the memory of the Nakba, the 1948 catastrophe that saw hundreds of thousands of Palestinians displaced from their homes. For the younger generation, it is the fight for a future free from occupation.

Fatima, a grandmother in Gaza, reflects on her life: "I have seen much in my years. I have seen homes destroyed, families torn apart, but I have also seen love, unity, and strength. My children and grandchildren will never forget their heritage. They will never forget that we are Palestinians, and we will always fight for our rights."

The World's Failure to Recognize Resilience

Despite their resilience, the Palestinian people are often ignored or misunderstood by the international community. Their struggle is reduced to a political conflict rather than a fight for basic human rights.

Yet, it is important to recognize that resilience is not a substitute for justice. The world cannot continue to admire the Palestinian spirit without demanding an end to the occupation. True support for Palestine is not just about acknowledging their endurance, but about ensuring that their rights are upheld and their suffering ends.

Hope in the Face of Injustice

Palestinians continue to endure because they have no other choice. But their resilience is not a passive acceptance of their fate—it is a declaration that they will not be erased. They will fight, not with weapons, but with their unwavering commitment to their land, their families, and their identity.

As long as they breathe, the struggle will continue. And with each new generation, the flame of hope burns brighter, refusing to be extinguished.

#8 The Struggle for Identity: Preserving Palestinian Culture

A Nation Defined by Its Heritage

Palestine is more than a place on the map; it is a culture, a history, and a people bound together by shared memories and traditions. Despite years of occupation, the Palestinian identity remains fiercely intact, shaped by the land, the language, and the enduring spirit of its people. This identity is not just about surviving; it is about preserving what has always defined them in the face of adversity.

From the olive trees that have symbolized their connection to the land for generations, to the food, music, and art that carry the stories of their past, Palestinian culture is a testament to their resilience. It is a defiance against attempts to erase their heritage and a celebration of what it means to be Palestinian, even when the world often fails to recognize them as such.

The Role of Language

Language is one of the cornerstones of Palestinian identity. Arabic, with its rich history and deep connection to the land, is not just a means of communication but a symbol of resistance. Palestinian poets, writers, and scholars have long used their language to express the struggles, dreams, and hopes of their people.

For many Palestinians, speaking Arabic is an act of defiance. In an age where so much of their history is either ignored or misrepresented, the use of language becomes an assertion of their existence. The language itself carries the weight of their ancestors, their traditions, and their cultural pride.

The Symbolism of the Olive Tree

The olive tree is not only a symbol of peace but also of Palestinian identity. For centuries, olive farming has been a way of life for Palestinians, and the trees themselves are a living connection to the land. The olive tree has been passed down from one generation to the next, providing sustenance, shade, and a sense of belonging.

However, under the occupation, the olive tree has also become a symbol of resistance. Settlements, military operations, and land confiscations have led to the destruction of thousands of olive trees, yet Palestinians continue to plant and nurture them. "Even when they destroy our trees, they cannot erase our roots," says Ahmed, a farmer in the West Bank. "The olive tree will always be part of us."

Traditional Palestinian Clothing: A Symbol of Heritage

Palestinian embroidery is another expression of cultural resistance. The intricate designs, passed down through generations of women, reflect the unique history and traditions of different Palestinian villages. Each stitch, each color, carries a story of the land, the people, and the resilience that defines them.

In the bustling streets of Hebron, Fatima, an elderly woman, sits in front of her home, stitching a piece of traditional embroidery. "This art is our history," she says. "Every pattern tells the story of our village, of our lives before the occupation. Even if we lose our homes, we will never lose this."

Music and Dance: Voices of Resistance

Music and dance have always been central to Palestinian life. The traditional sounds of the oud, the darbuka, and the qanun have long been part of celebrations, protests, and the rhythms of daily life. In times of hardship, music has become a source of comfort, a way to express emotions that words cannot capture.

The national dance, the "Dabke," is another expression of cultural pride. Performed in groups, with synchronized steps and lively music, the Dabke is a symbol of unity, resilience, and the strength of Palestinian communities. It is danced in weddings, protests, and celebrations, a reminder that no matter the hardships they face, the Palestinian people will always stand together.

Palestinian Art: Defying the Narrative

Art has always been a means for Palestinians to express their experiences and challenge the dominant narratives that seek to undermine their history. From graffiti on the separation wall in Bethlehem to contemporary art exhibited in galleries around the world, Palestinian artists use their work to tell stories that are often ignored.

In the West Bank, Rana, a young artist, uses her paintings to capture the pain and beauty of life under occupation. "Through my art, I want the world to see our humanity," she says. "They want to erase us, but through our art, we will make sure our story is told."

The Struggle to Preserve Culture in Exile

For many Palestinians living in refugee camps, the struggle to preserve their cultural identity is compounded by their displacement. Forced to leave their homes decades ago, they have recreated their lives in camps scattered across the Middle East, from Lebanon to Jordan to Syria. Yet even in exile, they continue to hold on to their cultural practices, passing down traditions to younger generations who have never set foot on the land of Palestine.

In a refugee camp in Lebanon, Youssef, a father of three, tells his children the stories of Palestine. "Even though we are far from home, we carry our culture with us," he says. "You must always remember who you are. Palestine is not just a place; it is in our hearts."

The Fight for Cultural Recognition

While Palestinians strive to preserve their cultural heritage, they are also engaged in a fight for cultural recognition on the world stage. From UNESCO recognition of Palestinian heritage sites to the international celebration of Palestinian art, music, and literature, there is an ongoing effort to ensure that Palestinian culture is acknowledged and respected.

But this recognition often comes with challenges. The global influence of certain political powers has made it difficult for Palestinian culture to be celebrated without controversy. Despite these hurdles, Palestinians continue to assert their right to their culture, their history, and their identity.

A Culture Unbroken

Palestinian culture is not just a legacy; it is a living, breathing force that continues to evolve despite the hardships. It is a culture defined by resilience, by the refusal to forget, and by the determination to pass on to future generations the richness of what it means to be Palestinian.

As the occupation continues, and as the world watches in silence, the Palestinian people will not let their culture be forgotten. For in their heritage lies their strength—an unbreakable bond to the land, to each other, and to the future they continue to fight for.

#9 The International Struggle: Solidarity and Silence

A World Divided in Response

While Palestinians have long fought their battle for justice, their struggle has often been met with a complex, divided response from the international community. Some nations, organizations, and individuals have stood in solidarity with the Palestinian cause, demanding justice, freedom, and an end to the occupation. Others, however, have remained silent or even complicit, disregarding the cries for help as mere political noise.

For decades, international human rights organizations have documented the violations occurring in Palestine, from the demolition of homes to the expansion of settlements. Reports have detailed the horrific consequences of military actions on innocent civilians, the imprisonment of thousands without trial, and the ongoing displacement of Palestinians from their ancestral lands. Despite these records, the world's response has often been muted, slow, or inadequate.

The Role of the United Nations

The United Nations (UN) has played a significant role in attempting to address the Palestinian question, yet its effectiveness has often been questioned. Resolutions passed by the UN General Assembly, calling for the end of the occupation and the recognition of Palestinian statehood, have been largely ignored. While many countries support these resolutions, others—particularly powerful nations—have used their veto powers to block decisive action.

Resolution 242, passed in 1967, called for the withdrawal of Israeli forces from territories occupied during the Six-Day War, including the West Bank, Gaza Strip, and East Jerusalem. However, decades later, little progress has been made in implementing this resolution. The presence of settlements and the expansion of Israeli control over Palestinian territories continue unabated, despite international condemnation.

Global Movements for Palestinian Solidarity

Despite the international community's inability to impose lasting peace, grassroots movements and activists around the world have taken it upon themselves to raise awareness about the Palestinian struggle. Campaigns like the Boycott, Divestment, and Sanctions (BDS) movement have gained traction, urging governments, corporations, and institutions to stop supporting businesses and products linked to the Israeli occupation.

In cities across Europe, the Americas, and Asia, Palestinians and their allies have organized protests, demonstrations, and public campaigns. These events have brought global attention to the injustices taking place in Palestine, calling for an end to the occupation and for the recognition of Palestinian rights. These movements have become an important part of the fight for justice, providing a voice for Palestinians in the face of official silence.

The Power of Media and Social Networks

In the modern age, social media has played an essential role in amplifying the Palestinian voice. Platforms like Twitter, Facebook, Instagram, and TikTok have allowed Palestinians to share their stories, their suffering, and their resistance with the world. Videos of protests, images of destroyed homes, and stories of families torn apart have flooded the digital landscape, reaching millions globally.

This digital mobilization has also been crucial in bypassing traditional media channels, which at times have either misrepresented or failed to fully cover the Palestinian plight. Hashtags such as #FreePalestine and #SaveSheikhJarrah have sparked viral campaigns, raising awareness of the ongoing injustices faced by Palestinians, especially during moments of heightened violence, such as military offensives or evictions from East Jerusalem neighborhoods.

But the power of social media has also faced backlash. Platforms have been accused of censorship, removing content that supports the Palestinian cause or condemns Israeli actions. Despite this, the Palestinian voice continues to grow louder in the digital realm, reaching hearts and minds across borders.

Complicity and Silence of the Powerful

One of the most significant challenges in the Palestinian struggle is the complicity and silence of powerful nations. The United States, in particular, has been a key ally of Israel for decades, providing both military and diplomatic support. This relationship has had a profound impact on the international community's response to the conflict, often overshadowing the plight of the Palestinian people.

While other countries, such as those in Europe, have occasionally voiced their concerns over the treatment of Palestinians, their actions have frequently been at odds with their words. Economic ties, military partnerships, and political alliances have often influenced their response, or lack thereof, to the situation in Palestine.

The silence of many powerful nations in the face of human rights abuses has created an atmosphere where Palestinian suffering is frequently overlooked or justified. The imbalance of power in the international system, where geopolitical interests often take precedence over justice, has kept Palestine in a state of perpetual struggle.

The Growing Role of Civil Society and Humanitarian Organizations

Amidst political inaction, civil society organizations and humanitarian groups have stepped in to fill the void. International organizations like Amnesty International, Human Rights Watch, and the International Committee of the Red Cross have consistently reported on the violations of Palestinian rights. These groups work to provide aid to Palestinians in the occupied territories and refugee camps, while also pressuring governments to take action.

These humanitarian efforts are vital to the survival of many Palestinians, offering medical assistance, food, and support to those who have suffered the most from the occupation. Despite the challenges they face in accessing the region, these organizations have continued to provide critical services, making an impact in the lives of thousands of people who otherwise would have no recourse.

However, even humanitarian work has faced political roadblocks, with organizations being accused of bias or being targeted for their support of Palestinian rights. This further complicates the global response to Palestine, as humanitarian efforts are often entangled in the broader political discourse.

The Future of Palestinian Struggle and Global Solidarity

The future of the Palestinian struggle is uncertain, but the continued efforts of solidarity movements, civil society, and the Palestinian people themselves are critical. As the global community becomes more aware of the situation, there is hope that greater pressure will be placed on governments and international bodies to hold Israel accountable for its actions.

The role of the international community in achieving peace and justice for Palestinians cannot be underestimated. True solidarity requires more than just words; it requires action. It requires a shift away from silence and complicity and toward a commitment to justice, equality, and human rights for all.

A Call to Action

In the end, the struggle for Palestine is not just a regional issue—it is a global one. It is a struggle for human dignity, for justice, and for the basic rights of people who have suffered for far too long. The international community must stand with Palestinians, not out of charity or sympathy, but because justice demands it. Silence is complicity, and it is time for the world to speak out.

It is time to recognize that the struggle for Palestine is a struggle for humanity itself.

#10 The Heart of Palestine: Resilience Amidst Despair

A People's Indomitable Spirit

Despite the harshest of conditions, the spirit of the Palestinian people remains unbroken. For decades, they have lived under occupation, enduring violence, displacement, and deprivation. Yet, amid the rubble of bombed-out homes, in the shadow of walls that separate families, and beneath the oppressive weight of military control, the resilience of Palestinians continues to shine.

In cities, villages, and refugee camps, Palestinians hold on to their identity, their heritage, and their hope for a future free from occupation. From the elderly who recount stories of a land untouched by war to the youth who dream of a life beyond the confines of military checkpoints, the Palestinian struggle is not just a fight for survival—it is a fight for dignity, for justice, and for the right to live as free people in their own land.

The Role of Culture in Resistance

Culture has been one of the greatest tools of resistance for the Palestinian people. Music, art, literature, and poetry have become powerful symbols of defiance. They tell the story of a people who refuse to be erased, who refuse to forget their roots, and who continue to pass down the memory of their homeland to future generations.

Palestinian poetry, in particular, has become a significant form of resistance. Poets like Mahmoud Darwish have captured the essence of the Palestinian struggle in words, expressing the pain of exile, the longing for home, and the hope for freedom. Darwish's poetry resonates not only with Palestinians but with people around the world who find themselves fighting for justice.

In the face of oppression, Palestinian art and culture have flourished as symbols of strength, unity, and defiance. Through their works, Palestinians have shown that even in the most dire circumstances, their identity cannot be stripped away. Their culture is a living testament to their resistance and their determination to preserve their heritage.

The Importance of Education and Knowledge

In the midst of adversity, education remains a pillar of Palestinian resistance. Despite the destruction of schools and the challenges of living under occupation, Palestinians have placed a high value on education, seeing it as a means of empowerment and a way to preserve their future.

Palestinian universities and schools continue to produce scholars, thinkers, and activists who contribute to the global conversation on human rights, justice, and liberation. The Palestinian education system, though limited and often disrupted by conflict, has created a generation of young people who are not only knowledgeable but also deeply committed to the cause of freedom.

Many Palestinian students have excelled abroad, earning degrees and using their education to advocate for their homeland. These individuals have become ambassadors for Palestine, spreading awareness about the occupation and amplifying the voices of those who are silenced within the occupied territories.

The Role of Women in the Struggle

Palestinian women have always played a central role in the resistance. From the early days of the struggle for independence to the ongoing battle against occupation, Palestinian women have been at the forefront, organizing protests, leading social movements, and supporting their communities. They have been mothers, daughters, and sisters who have borne the brunt of the occupation, but they have also been warriors—fighting for their rights, their families, and their land.

Palestinian women have faced unimaginable hardship, from losing loved ones in conflict to witnessing the destruction of their homes. Yet, despite these challenges, they continue to inspire with their strength and resilience. Many women have become leaders in the political and social movements, advocating for peace, justice, and equality for all Palestinians.

The Youth of Palestine: The Future of the Struggle

The youth of Palestine are perhaps the most vital force in the ongoing struggle for liberation. Growing up in an environment shaped by occupation, displacement, and conflict, Palestinian youth are acutely aware of the injustice they face. Yet, rather than succumbing to despair, many young Palestinians are channeling their anger and frustration into activism, striving to change the narrative and to create a better future for their people.

The Palestinian youth have embraced technology as a tool for activism, using social media to share their stories, organize protests, and mobilize international solidarity. They have created a digital revolution that amplifies their voices and challenges the international community to pay attention to their plight.

In addition to political activism, the youth of Palestine are also focused on preserving their culture and identity. Through music, art, and storytelling, they continue to honor the legacy of their ancestors, passing on the message of resistance and hope.

The Refugees: The Long Road to Return

Perhaps the most heartbreaking aspect of the Palestinian struggle is the fate of the refugees. Over 70 years have passed since the Nakba, yet millions of Palestinians still live in refugee camps in the Middle East, waiting for the day they can return to their homeland.

The refugees' right to return is a fundamental part of the Palestinian cause. It is a right that has been enshrined in international law, yet it remains denied by Israel. The Palestinian refugees have maintained their sense of identity, preserving the memory of their homes, their villages, and their land. They pass down stories to their children and grandchildren, ensuring that the dream of return is never forgotten.

For the Palestinian refugees, the struggle is not just about surviving in exile; it is about returning home. It is about reclaiming what was lost and finding justice for the generations that were uprooted from their land. The Palestinian refugee issue remains one of the core challenges in any peace process, and it is a matter of immense emotional significance for the entire Palestinian nation.

Hope Amidst the Darkness

Despite the challenges and the overwhelming obstacles, there is a deep well of hope that sustains the Palestinian people. It is a hope that refuses to die, even in the face of years of occupation and suffering. It is the hope of return, of freedom, of justice, and of a future where Palestinians can live in peace and dignity in their own land.

That hope is nourished by the love of family, the strength of community, and the unshakable belief that one day, Palestine will be free. It is a hope that has been passed down from generation to generation, from the Nakba to the present day. And as long as that hope remains alive, the struggle will continue.

The Path Forward

The road ahead is long and fraught with challenges, but the spirit of Palestine remains unwavering. The international community, if it chooses to act, can play a crucial role in helping to bring about peace and justice for Palestinians. But the ultimate responsibility lies with the Palestinian people themselves, who continue to fight for their rights, their land, and their future.

The resilience of the Palestinian people, in all its forms, is a beacon of hope. It is a reminder that even in the darkest moments, the human spirit can endure. And as long as there is hope, there is the possibility for change.

#11 The Global Struggle: Solidarity and the Fight for Justice

The Role of International Solidarity

While the struggle for Palestine has been a deeply internal one, fought primarily by the Palestinians themselves, it has also been a global issue—one that has drawn the attention, support, and sometimes the opposition of countries and movements worldwide. Solidarity with Palestine has been a cornerstone of the struggle, with individuals, organizations, and governments rallying to the cause of justice for the Palestinian people.

From the early days of the Palestinian refugee crisis to the present, international solidarity movements have consistently challenged the occupation, the settlements, and the systemic oppression faced by Palestinians. From anti-apartheid activists to human rights organizations, the global community has long recognized the injustice of the Palestinian situation and rallied to change the narrative.

Many global movements have supported the Boycott, Divestment, and Sanctions (BDS) campaign, an effort to pressure Israel through economic, cultural, and academic means to end its violations of international law. Through this and other campaigns, international solidarity has helped to amplify the Palestinian voice and raise awareness of the issues at the heart of the conflict.

However, the international response has not always been one of support. Many Western governments, particularly the United States, have consistently sided with Israel, often providing political, military, and economic backing. This alliance has further entrenched the occupation and prevented meaningful progress toward peace.

Despite this, the growing global solidarity movement continues to push for change and demand that the international community stand up for the rights of Palestinians.

The Media's Role: Telling the Truth

The role of the media in shaping the Palestinian narrative cannot be overstated. For years, the stories of Palestinian suffering, displacement, and resistance were marginalized, with much of the global media framing the situation as a "conflict" between two equal sides. This portrayal obscured the reality of occupation and the vast power imbalance between the oppressor and the oppressed.

In recent years, however, alternative media platforms, independent journalists, and social media movements have helped shift the narrative. The rise of citizen journalism, where Palestinians themselves have taken to social media to document their lives, struggles, and aspirations, has been a powerful tool in exposing the reality of occupation to the wider world.

Images and videos of the destruction in Gaza, the violence against Palestinian protesters, and the daily life under occupation have gone viral, bringing the realities of Palestine into living rooms and smartphones across the globe. These raw, unfiltered glimpses into Palestinian life have made it increasingly difficult for the international community to ignore the suffering of the Palestinian people.

At the same time, Palestinian activists and journalists have faced immense pressure from both Israeli authorities and the international community. Many have been arrested, silenced, or censored for their efforts to tell the truth. Yet, despite these efforts to suppress their voices, the Palestinian struggle continues to find its way to the global stage.

The Fight for Recognition and Statehood

One of the central issues in the Palestinian struggle has been the demand for recognition as a sovereign state. Since the creation of Israel in 1948, Palestinians have been denied the right to self-determination and have been subjected to occupation, land theft, and displacement.

Over the years, Palestinians have sought recognition from the international community for their right to establish an independent state in the territories that were promised to them under international law. The Palestinian Liberation Organization (PLO) has worked tirelessly to garner support for Palestinian statehood, engaging in diplomacy with other countries, securing recognition from dozens of nations, and pushing for a resolution at the United Nations.

Despite these efforts, the road to full recognition and statehood has been fraught with obstacles. Israel's continued expansion of settlements on Palestinian land, the division of the Palestinian territories between the West Bank and Gaza, and the failure of peace talks have all contributed to the continued denial of Palestinian sovereignty.

The international community, while recognizing Palestine as a non-member observer state in the United Nations in 2012, has not been able to secure a fair and lasting solution to the question of Palestinian statehood. The failure to achieve a two-state solution, one of the long-standing goals of the peace process, remains a critical barrier to peace in the region.

The Role of Youth and Grassroots Movements

In the face of political inaction and continued occupation, many Palestinians have turned to grassroots movements and youth-led organizations as a means of achieving change. These movements, often unrecognized by mainstream political structures, have become a powerful force for mobilization, education, and advocacy.

Palestinian youth, in particular, have been at the forefront of these movements. As the generation that has grown up under occupation, they have experienced firsthand the limitations of traditional political solutions and have sought alternative avenues to bring about change. Through organizing protests, engaging in direct action, and using digital platforms to spread awareness, Palestinian youth have become a driving force for resistance.

One of the most notable grassroots movements in recent years has been the Great Return March, which began in Gaza in 2018. Thousands of Palestinians participated in weekly protests along the border with Israel, demanding the right to return to their homes and calling for an end to the blockade on Gaza. Though the protests were met with violence from Israeli forces, the movement demonstrated the power of collective action and the resilience of the Palestinian people.

These grassroots movements have also played a crucial role in educating the broader public about the Palestinian cause. By sharing their stories and experiences, Palestinians have been able to humanize the struggle and call for greater international action. As these movements continue to grow, they are shaping the future of Palestinian resistance and creating a new generation of activists committed to achieving justice.

The Moral Imperative: Why the World Must Act

The struggle for Palestine is not just a political issue; it is a moral one. The question of Palestinian rights is a question of human rights. For over seven decades, the Palestinian people have suffered under occupation, discrimination, and violence. The international community, particularly the United Nations, has repeatedly condemned Israel's actions, yet little concrete action has been taken to hold Israel accountable for its violations of international law.

The time has come for the world to step up and demand justice for the Palestinian people. The continued denial of Palestinian rights cannot be justified. The international community must take a stand for peace, for equality, and for the recognition of Palestinian sovereignty.

The question is no longer whether the world should act—it is whether the international community will have the courage to do so. It is a question of standing on the right side of history, of choosing justice over indifference, and of upholding the principles of human dignity and freedom for all.

#12 A Vision for Peace: The Path Forward

The Dream of Peace

In the midst of conflict, there is a dream that continues to persist— a dream of peace, coexistence, and justice. This vision has been shared by generations of Palestinians and their allies, yet it remains elusive, obscured by decades of violence, failed peace talks, and political impasse. Nevertheless, the dream persists, because without it, there is no reason to endure, to resist, to strive for a better future.

The dream is simple: a world where Palestinians and Israelis can live side by side in peace, with mutual respect and recognition of each other's rights. It is a vision of a Palestinian state that exists within the borders of 1967, with East Jerusalem as its capital, as enshrined by international law and numerous United Nations resolutions. It is a dream of an end to the occupation, of freedom for Palestinian refugees to return to their ancestral lands, and of an end to the blockade on Gaza.

However, this dream is not just a political one—it is a moral one. It is about justice, dignity, and the right to live free from oppression. It is about recognizing the humanity of the other, not as enemies but as equals. It is a vision that calls on the international community to stand up for what is right, not for what is politically convenient.

The Obstacles to Peace

Achieving peace in Palestine has proven to be a daunting challenge. Numerous peace plans, from the Oslo Accords to the Road Map for Peace, have been proposed, but none have brought about a lasting solution. The reasons for this failure are multifaceted and complex.

One major obstacle is the ongoing expansion of Israeli settlements in the occupied West Bank. These settlements, deemed illegal under international law, have continued to grow despite repeated calls for a halt to their construction. The expansion of settlements not only undermines the prospects for a two-state solution but also deepens the sense of injustice felt by Palestinians who see their land being systematically taken from them.

Another major obstacle is the division between the Palestinian factions. The rivalry between Fatah, which controls the West Bank, and Hamas, which governs Gaza, has long been a source of instability within Palestinian politics. This division has hampered efforts for unity and has created a fractured Palestinian leadership, making it difficult to present a united front in negotiations with Israel.

Additionally, the continued violence and acts of terrorism on both sides of the conflict have perpetuated a cycle of fear, hatred, and distrust. The toll of this violence is felt not only in the immediate loss of life but in the long-term psychological scars it leaves on both Israelis and Palestinians. This ongoing trauma makes it difficult for either side to envision a future in which peace is possible.

The Role of the International Community

The international community has a crucial role to play in bringing about peace in Palestine. Over the years, countries and organizations have proposed various solutions, but it is clear that no lasting peace can be achieved without the active involvement of the global community. The United Nations, the European Union, and other international bodies must put pressure on both sides to come to the negotiating table, to uphold international law, and to commit to a just and fair peace.

The international community must also hold Israel accountable for its violations of Palestinian rights. The continued occupation of Palestinian land, the illegal settlements, the blockade of Gaza, and the collective punishment of Palestinians must be condemned and brought to an end. At the same time, Palestinians must be encouraged to engage in dialogue and negotiations in good faith, with the recognition that peace can only be achieved through mutual understanding and compromise.

A New Approach: Beyond the Two-State Solution?

For decades, the two-state solution has been the cornerstone of international diplomacy regarding Palestine. The idea of an independent Palestinian state living side by side with Israel has been the goal of many peace initiatives, yet the continued expansion of settlements and the lack of progress in negotiations have led many to question whether this vision is still viable.

Some critics argue that the two-state solution is no longer feasible, given the current realities on the ground. They point to the fragmentation of Palestinian territories, the continued Israeli occupation, and the increasing difficulty of dividing Jerusalem as obstacles that make the two-state solution increasingly unlikely.

As a result, there are growing calls for alternative approaches to peace. Some advocates propose a one-state solution, in which Israelis and Palestinians live together in a single, democratic state with equal rights for all. Others advocate for a confederation of Israel and Palestine, in which both peoples share sovereignty over the land but maintain separate governments.

While these alternative solutions remain contentious, they reflect the frustration felt by many who see the two-state solution as a failed promise. Ultimately, the path to peace will require bold, new thinking and a willingness to challenge old assumptions about what is possible.

The Role of Palestinians in Shaping Their Future

While the international community has a significant role to play, it is the Palestinian people themselves who will ultimately shape their future. The resilience and determination of Palestinians in the face of adversity is nothing short of inspiring. Whether in the refugee camps of Lebanon, the streets of Gaza, or the villages of the West Bank, Palestinians continue to fight for their rights, for their dignity, and for their freedom.

The Palestinian leadership must prioritize unity and cooperation, putting aside internal divisions in favor of a collective strategy for peace. The days of infighting must be replaced with a renewed commitment to a shared goal: the liberation of Palestine and the realization of a just and lasting peace.

At the same time, Palestinian civil society has been a driving force for change. From grassroots movements to youth-led activism, Palestinians have consistently demonstrated their ability to organize, resist, and advocate for their rights. These movements must be supported and strengthened, as they represent the future of Palestine.

A Call for Justice and Freedom

As we look to the future, the call for justice and freedom rings louder than ever. The Palestinian people have waited long enough for a peace that acknowledges their rights, their history, and their aspirations. The time for a just peace is now.

Peace is not just the absence of war—it is the presence of justice, equality, and dignity. A lasting peace in Palestine will only be achieved when Palestinians are free to live on their own land, in their own state, with the rights and freedoms they deserve. It will come when Israel recognizes the humanity of the Palestinian people and works to build a future of coexistence, rather than perpetuating a cycle of violence and oppression.

As the world watches, it is time for all of us to take action. The struggle for Palestine is the struggle for justice, and it is a struggle that belongs to all of us. It is time to demand that peace, freedom, and dignity be granted to every Palestinian, for it is only through these values that a lasting peace can be achieved.

#13 The Struggle for Recognition and Identity

The Essence of Palestinian Identity

Palestinian identity is not merely a matter of land or politics— it is a deep-rooted sense of belonging, of history, and of an enduring connection to the land. For generations, Palestinians have held on to their heritage despite the constant threat of displacement, violence, and the erosion of their cultural identity. From the olive trees that have symbolized the Palestinian connection to the earth, to the traditional foods, music, and crafts that have passed down through generations, Palestinian identity remains resilient, despite efforts to suppress it.

This identity is not defined solely by the borders of a state or the reality of occupation, but by the lived experiences of millions of Palestinians, who continue to carry their culture, language, and memories with them wherever they go. Whether in the refugee camps of Jordan, Lebanon, and Syria, or the diaspora scattered around the world, Palestinians have managed to keep their identity alive. It is not defined by the state of Israel or any other external force, but by the collective will of a people who refuse to be erased from history.

However, this struggle for identity is not without its challenges. The continuous occupation, the displacement of families, and the destruction of Palestinian villages have caused irreparable damage to many aspects of Palestinian life. The loss of homes, family members, and the sense of normalcy has created a diaspora of displaced Palestinians, whose collective memory remains their only link to a homeland they may never return to. Yet, even in exile, Palestinians maintain a sense of pride in their heritage, an unwavering belief that their struggle for freedom will one day return them to their land.

The Quest for Recognition

Recognition is perhaps one of the most fundamental struggles faced by Palestinians today. The question of whether the Palestinian people and their rights are recognized by the international community remains central to the conflict. For many Palestinians, recognition is not just a political act— it is the acknowledgment of their humanity, their history, and their right to self-determination.

The Palestinian quest for recognition on the global stage has been long and fraught with challenges. Despite numerous declarations and resolutions from the United Nations calling for the recognition of Palestine as an independent state, the international community has remained divided. While many countries have recognized Palestine as a sovereign state, Israel and its allies, along with some powerful international organizations, continue to deny Palestinians the full recognition they seek.

This denial of recognition is not just about politics; it is about the erasure of a people's history, culture, and identity. When one's existence is not recognized, it becomes all the more difficult to build a future. For Palestinians, the lack of recognition by Israel and many parts of the world continues to fuel feelings of injustice, and without it, there is no path to peace.

International Recognition: A Double-Edged Sword?

While international recognition of Palestine has been a goal for many Palestinians and their supporters, it has often come with complications. On the one hand, recognition is crucial in asserting the legitimacy of the Palestinian cause. International recognition provides Palestinians with a platform to advocate for their rights and gain support from the global community. It also serves as a means to push back against the occupation and to claim Palestine's rightful place in the international order.

On the other hand, recognition without real change on the ground has often proven to be a hollow victory. While the Palestinian Authority has received recognition from various governments and organizations, this recognition has done little to alleviate the suffering of the Palestinian people. The occupation continues, settlements expand, and Palestinians remain without the basic rights they deserve.

Thus, recognition alone does not guarantee justice or freedom. It must be accompanied by real action to end the occupation, provide Palestinians with their full rights, and ensure a just peace. The international community must not only recognize Palestine but also take concrete steps to hold Israel accountable for its violations of Palestinian rights and to support a peaceful resolution based on justice and equality.

The Role of the Palestinian Diaspora

The Palestinian diaspora has played a critical role in the struggle for recognition and identity. Millions of Palestinians live outside the occupied territories, yet their connection to Palestine remains strong. The diaspora has been a powerful force for advocacy, raising awareness about the Palestinian cause and mobilizing support for Palestinian rights around the world.

Through organizations, grassroots movements, and social media, Palestinians in the diaspora have kept the plight of their people alive in the global consciousness. The Palestinian diaspora is also an essential part of the resistance—through protests, campaigns, and lobbying efforts, they continue to demand justice and equality for Palestinians. Their voices are vital in the global push for the recognition of Palestinian rights and the end of the occupation.

However, the diaspora also faces its own set of challenges. While they may be far from home, the Palestinian diaspora feels a profound sense of loss and displacement. Many have lived for generations in refugee camps or as displaced persons, holding on to the hope of one day returning to their homeland. This sense of exile is a source of both pain and strength, as it has fostered a collective identity that transcends borders and keeps the struggle for Palestine alive.

Palestinian Resistance: From Cultural Preservation to Political Struggle

Palestinian resistance is not just about armed struggle—it is a multifaceted movement that encompasses everything from cultural preservation to political activism. Palestinians have resisted the occupation in countless ways, from nonviolent protests and boycotts to armed resistance. But at its core, Palestinian resistance is about preserving a way of life, a culture, and an identity that has been under threat for decades.

Cultural resistance has been one of the most powerful tools Palestinians have at their disposal. Through music, art, literature, and folklore, Palestinians have continued to assert their identity in the face of oppression. Palestinian artists and writers have produced works that tell the story of their people's struggle, keeping alive the memory of their history and their connection to the land.

Political resistance, too, has been a central part of the Palestinian struggle. The Palestinian Liberation Organization (PLO) and other groups have fought for Palestinian independence and the right to self-determination, while seeking to raise awareness of the plight of the Palestinian people on the international stage. Resistance has come in many forms, from violent uprisings to peaceful protests, but the ultimate goal has always been the same: to end the occupation and establish a free, independent Palestinian state.

The resilience of Palestinian culture and resistance to occupation are the cornerstone of the Palestinian identity. They are proof that, despite all the obstacles, the Palestinian people will not be erased from history. Their identity, their culture, and their struggle for freedom will continue, until the day they can return to their homeland in peace.

#14 The Path of Resistance

Resilience in the Face of Adversity

Palestinian resistance is more than just a series of protests or conflicts—it is a deep, unyielding force that has shaped the Palestinian people for generations. Born from the harsh realities of occupation and the denial of basic rights, resistance in Palestine has taken many forms, from armed struggle to cultural preservation, from political activism to acts of everyday defiance. It is a powerful testament to the strength of the Palestinian spirit.

The path of resistance is never easy. It is filled with sacrifice, hardship, and often violence. But for Palestinians, it is the only path that ensures the survival of their identity, culture, and hope for a future in their homeland. Resistance is not merely an act of opposition—it is an assertion of existence in the face of forces that seek to erase the Palestinian people from the map, both literally and figuratively.

Every generation of Palestinians has contributed to this ongoing struggle. From the first Palestinian uprising in 1936 to the more recent Intifadas, the struggle for liberation has been passed down, continually adapted to changing circumstances. The resistance has included everything from grassroots protests against Israeli military actions, to campaigns for international recognition, to the creation of safe spaces where Palestinians can continue to live according to their traditions, even in exile.

The Armed Struggle

For some Palestinians, resistance has meant taking up arms against the occupation. Armed struggle has been a controversial but integral part of the Palestinian resistance movement, particularly during the early years of the Israeli occupation. Groups like the Palestine Liberation Organization (PLO), Hamas, and others have engaged in armed resistance as a means of confronting Israel's military dominance and its continued expansion of settlements on Palestinian land.

While some view armed resistance as a legitimate response to the violence and oppression Palestinians face, others argue that violence only perpetuates the cycle of suffering for both sides. Regardless of the approach, it is undeniable that the use of force has been a major element of the Palestinian resistance for decades.

The choice of armed resistance, however, does not come without its costs. Thousands of Palestinian lives have been lost in conflicts, and entire families have been displaced as a result of military operations. The trauma of war is passed down through generations, leaving physical and emotional scars on the Palestinian people. Yet, for many, the continuation of armed resistance is seen as an act of self-preservation and an effort to reclaim their dignity.

Nonviolent Resistance and International Solidarity

In contrast to armed resistance, nonviolent resistance has also been a key part of the Palestinian struggle. Nonviolent protests, strikes, and civil disobedience have long been central to the Palestinian movement, and many Palestinians continue to fight for their rights through peaceful means.

The Great March of Return, which began in 2018, is a striking example of nonviolent resistance. Palestinians from Gaza gathered along the border with Israel to demand the right to return to their homes and to protest against the continued Israeli occupation. Despite the peaceful nature of the protests, they were met with violent repression from Israeli forces, who responded with live ammunition, resulting in hundreds of Palestinian deaths and thousands of injuries.

This tragedy highlights a crucial paradox in the Palestinian resistance movement. Nonviolent protests are met with violence, which only reinforces the belief that Palestinians have no other option but to resort to armed struggle. The cycle of violence continues, and the Palestinian people remain caught between the desire for peace and the reality of their occupation.

International solidarity plays a significant role in Palestinian nonviolent resistance. Around the world, activists have worked to raise awareness of the Palestinian cause through campaigns, boycotts, and protests. The Boycott, Divestment, and Sanctions (BDS) movement has gained momentum in recent years, calling for global action against Israeli policies toward Palestine. International efforts like these are vital in amplifying the Palestinian struggle and providing solidarity to those who continue to resist in the occupied territories.

The Role of Women in the Resistance

Palestinian women have played an integral role in the resistance, from the early days of the struggle to the present. Women in Palestine have not only fought for their rights and equality but have also been active participants in the broader national struggle for freedom. Throughout history, women have been at the forefront of organizing protests, engaging in acts of civil disobedience, and providing support to prisoners and martyrs.

During the First Intifada, Palestinian women were instrumental in organizing boycotts of Israeli goods and in setting up underground networks to help support families affected by the occupation. Many Palestinian women have also joined armed resistance groups or become political leaders, challenging both the Israeli occupation and patriarchal structures within Palestinian society.

The role of women in the resistance is often underappreciated, yet their contributions are crucial to the continued fight for freedom. They have not only resisted occupation but have also fought for gender equality and the advancement of women's rights in Palestine. Their resilience is a powerful reminder that the struggle for liberation is not just about political power—it is about the dignity and rights of all people, regardless of gender.

The Price of Resistance

No path of resistance is without its sacrifices, and for the Palestinian people, the cost of this struggle has been tremendous. From the loss of life to the destruction of homes, from the trauma of war to the emotional toll of displacement, Palestinians continue to endure hardship after hardship. Yet, their commitment to resistance remains unwavering.

For many Palestinians, the price of resistance is not just material—it is emotional and psychological. Families are torn apart, with fathers, sons, and brothers imprisoned or killed, and mothers left to pick up the pieces. The collective trauma of occupation is passed down through generations, creating a sense of loss and grief that seems never-ending. Yet, despite these challenges, the Palestinian people continue to fight—not only for their freedom but for the future of their children.

The resilience of the Palestinian people in the face of such immense challenges is nothing short of extraordinary. It is a testament to the strength of the human spirit and the will to survive against all odds. In the face of unimaginable suffering, Palestinians have refused to surrender their identity, their culture, or their dreams of a free Palestine.

#15 Children of Conflict

The Lost Childhoods of Palestine

In a land where peace remains elusive, the greatest victims are often the youngest. For Palestinian children, growing up in the shadow of occupation means facing a harsh reality shaped by violence, displacement, and fear. Their laughter, innocence, and dreams are stolen by a conflict that they neither started nor understand, leaving scars that linger far beyond childhood.

Children in Palestine are born into a world of checkpoints, military raids, and blockades. Many have never known a day of peace, with their formative years defined by bombings, arrests, and the constant threat of displacement. The sound of drones overhead becomes a normal backdrop to their lives, while stories of loved ones lost to the conflict are part of their everyday conversations.

Education Under Siege

Education, a fundamental right of every child, is not exempt from the impacts of the occupation. Schools in the West Bank and Gaza are often targeted during military operations, and students are forced to navigate checkpoints or endure harassment on their way to class. In some areas, classrooms have been repurposed as shelters during times of heightened conflict, leaving children to study amid the ruins of their former lives.

Despite these challenges, Palestinian children demonstrate an extraordinary commitment to learning. Education is seen not just as a means of personal growth, but as an act of resistance—a way to preserve their culture and build a future in defiance of the forces that seek to suppress them.

Organizations and communities work tirelessly to keep schools functioning, even in the most challenging circumstances. Teachers often serve as mentors, counselors, and protectors, ensuring that children continue to learn and dream, despite the chaos around them.

The Psychological Toll

The emotional and psychological impact of growing up in a warzone cannot be overstated. Many Palestinian children experience symptoms of post-traumatic stress disorder (PTSD), anxiety, and depression as a result of the violence they witness and endure. The sight of demolished homes, the loss of family members, and the constant fear of raids leave deep, invisible wounds.

The lack of mental health support exacerbates the issue. While some non-governmental organizations and international bodies provide psychological aid, the overwhelming need far exceeds the resources available. As a result, many children are left to cope with their trauma alone, their pain becoming part of the collective grief of their people.

Dreams Amid Despair

Despite the overwhelming adversity, Palestinian children continue to dream. They dream of becoming doctors, engineers, teachers, and artists. They imagine a world where they can play freely in the streets, where their families can live without fear, and where their homeland is no longer a battleground.

These dreams are a source of hope—not just for the children themselves, but for the entire Palestinian community. They remind the world that even in the darkest of times, the human spirit remains unbroken.

The World's Responsibility

The plight of Palestinian children calls for urgent international attention. It is a moral imperative for the global community to protect the most vulnerable and ensure their rights to safety, education, and a childhood free from fear. Beyond political debates and geopolitical strategies, the suffering of children should serve as a rallying cry for humanity to act.

Peace may seem like a distant hope, but the future of Palestine depends on it. By investing in the well-being and education of its children, the seeds of a brighter tomorrow can be planted. The world owes it to these children to amplify their voices, share their stories, and work toward a future where no child has to grow up under the shadow of conflict.

#16 The Displaced and the Forgotten

A Nation Without a Homeland

For over seven decades, displacement has been the defining experience for millions of Palestinians. Expelled from their homes during the Nakba of 1948, many families fled with nothing but the clothes on their backs and the keys to houses they hoped to one day return to. These keys, passed down through generations, have become powerful symbols of hope and loss—reminders of the homes that now exist only in memory.

The Palestinian refugee crisis is one of the longest-running in modern history. Today, millions of Palestinians live as refugees in countries like Jordan, Lebanon, and Syria, or in camps within Gaza and the West Bank. Their lives are marked by statelessness, poverty, and a yearning for the land they still call home.

The Refugee Camps

Refugee camps, intended as temporary shelters, have become semi-permanent settlements over the decades. In these camps, overcrowding, inadequate infrastructure, and limited resources are the norm. The streets are narrow, the buildings hastily constructed, and the air thick with the collective weight of unfulfilled dreams.

Life in the camps is a daily struggle for survival. Access to clean water, healthcare, and education is often limited, and unemployment rates are staggeringly high. Yet, even in these dire circumstances, Palestinian refugees persevere. Communities come together to support one another, preserving their culture and identity against all odds.

Stories of the Displaced

Every Palestinian refugee carries a story—of the land they left, the hardships they endured, and the dreams they hold onto. For many, these stories are all they have left of their past. Elders recount tales of olive groves and bustling markets, painting vivid pictures of the homeland for younger generations who have never seen it.

These stories are more than just memories; they are acts of resistance. By keeping their history alive, Palestinians assert their identity and refuse to let the world forget their struggle.

The Right of Return

At the heart of the Palestinian struggle lies the demand for the right of return—a fundamental principle enshrined in international law but denied to Palestinians. The right of return is not just about reclaiming property; it is about justice, dignity, and the recognition of a people's right to live in their ancestral land.

This demand has been met with resistance, particularly from Israel, which views it as a threat to its demographic balance. Despite this, Palestinians continue to fight for their right to return, believing that without it, true peace and justice cannot be achieved.

The Forgotten Crisis

In a world inundated with crises, the plight of Palestinian refugees often fades into the background. International aid fluctuates with political priorities, leaving many refugees to rely on dwindling resources from organizations like UNRWA (United Nations Relief and Works Agency).

This neglect exacerbates the suffering of the displaced, pushing them further into the margins of society. The global community's indifference serves as a painful reminder of the challenges Palestinians face in their pursuit of justice.

Resilience Amid Despair

Despite the immense challenges, Palestinian refugees continue to demonstrate remarkable resilience. They build schools, start businesses, and create art that tells their story to the world. Their resilience is not born out of choice but necessity—a testament to the strength of the human spirit in the face of adversity.

A Call to Action

The plight of Palestinian refugees is not just a Palestinian issue; it is a global one. The international community has a moral obligation to address the root causes of their displacement and work toward a just and lasting solution. This means not only providing humanitarian aid but also supporting efforts for peace, justice, and the recognition of Palestinian rights.

The displaced and the forgotten deserve more than sympathy—they deserve action. The keys they hold are not just relics of the past; they are symbols of a future where they can return home, free from fear and oppression.

#17 The Silent Siege

Life Under Blockade

For over a decade, the Gaza Strip has endured a relentless blockade that has turned it into what many describe as an "open-air prison." The blockade, imposed by land, sea, and air, has crippled the region's economy, decimated infrastructure, and left over two million Palestinians struggling to survive under conditions that the United Nations has repeatedly deemed unlivable.

In Gaza, the most basic aspects of life—clean water, electricity, and medical care—are luxuries often out of reach. The blockade has restricted the flow of goods, from essential medicines to construction materials, leaving hospitals without supplies, schools without resources, and homes in ruins.

The Human Cost of Isolation

The blockade's impact extends far beyond economic deprivation; it has inflicted deep psychological and emotional wounds on Gaza's population. Trapped within a 365-square-kilometer strip of land, residents live with the constant fear of airstrikes, the trauma of past wars, and the despair of an uncertain future.

For the youth of Gaza, this isolation has been especially devastating. Many have never left the strip, growing up with no experience of the world beyond its borders. Dreams of pursuing higher education, careers, or simply traveling remain just that—dreams.

The Struggle for Survival

Despite the blockade, Gazans have found ways to survive, demonstrating extraordinary resilience and creativity. Fishermen venture into restricted waters, farmers cultivate crops under threat, and entrepreneurs find ways to innovate within severe constraints.

One example of this resilience is the emergence of grassroots initiatives that turn destruction into hope. Rubble from bombed buildings is recycled into construction materials, while small-scale solar projects provide electricity to communities cut off from the grid. These efforts are a testament to the enduring spirit of a people determined to live with dignity.

Healthcare in Crisis

The healthcare system in Gaza is on the brink of collapse. Hospitals are understaffed and under-equipped, with frequent power outages endangering the lives of patients. Specialized treatments, such as cancer therapy, are nearly impossible to access, forcing patients to seek permits to travel for care—permits that are often denied or delayed.

During escalations of violence, hospitals become overwhelmed with casualties, and medical professionals work tirelessly under unimaginable conditions. International aid organizations attempt to fill the gaps, but the scale of the crisis often exceeds their capacity.

The Environmental Toll

The blockade has also taken a severe toll on Gaza's environment. With limited access to clean water, many residents rely on contaminated sources, leading to widespread waterborne diseases. Untreated sewage flows into the Mediterranean, not only harming marine ecosystems but also endangering the health of those who depend on the sea for their livelihoods.

Efforts to address these issues are hampered by restrictions on importing materials needed for repairs and upgrades. As a result, environmental degradation continues to worsen, further jeopardizing the well-being of Gaza's population.

The International Response

While the international community has condemned the blockade, concrete action remains limited. Humanitarian aid provides temporary relief, but it does not address the root causes of Gaza's suffering. The silence and inaction of powerful nations allow the blockade to persist, perpetuating the cycle of poverty and despair.

Hope Amid Despair

Even in the face of immense adversity, hope persists in Gaza. Artists, writers, and activists use their talents to share their stories with the world, highlighting the humanity behind the headlines. Schools and community centers work tirelessly to provide education and support, nurturing a generation that refuses to be defined by the confines of the blockade.

The spirit of Gaza's people is unyielding, a testament to their unwavering determination to reclaim their rights and dignity. Their resilience serves as a reminder that even in the darkest of times, hope can thrive.

Breaking the Silence

The blockade of Gaza is not just a Palestinian tragedy; it is a stain on the conscience of the global community. It is a reminder that indifference and inaction have consequences, and that silence can be as damaging as complicity.

To break the siege, the world must not only address the immediate humanitarian needs but also work toward a just and lasting resolution to the conflict. Gaza deserves more than survival—it deserves freedom, prosperity, and peace.

#18 Children of Palestine

Growing Up in Conflict

For the children of Palestine, childhood is not defined by innocence but by survival. From a young age, they are thrust into a world of checkpoints, military raids, and the ever-present sound of drones. Playgrounds are replaced by rubble-strewn streets, and laughter is often stifled by the echoes of war.

These children have witnessed and endured what no child should— losing parents, siblings, and friends to violence, and growing up in an environment where fear and uncertainty overshadow their dreams. Yet, they persist, carrying the hopes of an entire nation on their small shoulders.

Education Under Occupation

Education is a lifeline for Palestinian children, a symbol of hope and a pathway to a better future. However, attending school is often fraught with danger. In the West Bank, children must navigate checkpoints and harassment by settlers to reach their classrooms. In Gaza, schools frequently become targets during military conflicts, leaving students and teachers in harm's way.

Despite these challenges, Palestinian children and their families prioritize education, viewing it as both a right and a form of resistance. Teachers in the region demonstrate remarkable dedication, often working under dire conditions to provide not just knowledge, but also a sense of normalcy and stability.

The Psychological Toll

The psychological impact of living in a conflict zone cannot be overstated. Many Palestinian children suffer from anxiety, depression, and post-traumatic stress disorder (PTSD). Nightmares, fear of loud noises, and difficulty concentrating are common among those who have experienced violence firsthand.

Organizations on the ground work tirelessly to provide psychosocial support, offering safe spaces for children to process their trauma through art, play, and storytelling. These initiatives are vital, but the long-term effects of such sustained stress remain a concern for an entire generation.

The Spirit of Resistance

Despite the hardships, Palestinian children embody resilience and resistance. Their artwork often depicts their dreams of peace and freedom, while their songs and poetry speak of a homeland they long to see liberated. Through their creativity and determination, they continue to inspire both their communities and the global audience.

Their resistance is not just about defying occupation; it is about preserving their identity and asserting their right to exist as a people. In every classroom, every song, and every drawing, the children of Palestine are building the foundations of hope.

A Future Worth Fighting For

The plight of Palestinian children is a stark reminder of the human cost of the conflict. They deserve more than survival; they deserve a future filled with opportunities, peace, and security. Ensuring that future requires global action to address the root causes of their suffering and to uphold their rights as enshrined in international law.

A Global Responsibility

The children of Palestine are not just the responsibility of their parents or their communities—they are the responsibility of the world. The international community must do more than express outrage; it must act decisively to protect their rights and provide them with the resources they need to thrive.

Investing in Palestinian children is not just an act of compassion; it is an investment in peace. By empowering them with education, mental health support, and opportunities, we can help break the cycle of violence and build a future where all children can live with dignity and hope.

#19 The Women of Palestine

Silent Strength, Loud Resistance

In the narrative of Palestine, women play a central yet often underrepresented role. They are the silent strength of their families and communities, holding together the fabric of society amidst the chaos of occupation and conflict. As mothers, daughters, educators, activists, and leaders, Palestinian women embody resilience and courage in the face of adversity.

Their resistance is multifaceted. Some take to the streets, leading protests against land confiscation or military raids. Others resist through education, ensuring their children grow up with the knowledge and pride of their heritage. In their homes, they create sanctuaries of normalcy, instilling hope and resilience in the next generation.

Living Under Double Oppression

Palestinian women endure a dual burden of oppression—one from the occupation and another from societal norms that often limit their roles. Checkpoints, curfews, and violence restrict their movements and access to resources, while traditional expectations can confine their voices within their communities.

Despite these challenges, Palestinian women have been at the forefront of the struggle for justice. Whether as organizers of grassroots movements or as caregivers ensuring the survival of their families, their contributions are indispensable.

Mothers of Resistance

The image of the Palestinian mother has become a symbol of endurance. Many have watched their sons and daughters taken away—some imprisoned, others martyred. Yet, they continue to fight for their children's right to live in dignity and freedom.

Through their grief, these women find strength, turning personal loss into a collective call for justice. Their stories are a testament to the unyielding spirit of Palestine, where even in the darkest moments, hope refuses to die.

Breaking Barriers

In recent years, Palestinian women have broken barriers in various fields, challenging stereotypes and asserting their place in society. They have become doctors, engineers, writers, and politicians, proving that even under occupation, ambition and talent cannot be silenced.

Their success stories resonate far beyond Palestine, inspiring women worldwide to stand up against oppression and pursue their dreams. Through their achievements, they shatter the image of Palestinians as merely victims, showcasing the potential and talent that thrive despite adversity.

Voices of Change

Palestinian women are not only participants but also leaders in the struggle for justice. Figures like Hanan Ashrawi, Leila Khaled, and countless unnamed activists have shown the world that Palestinian women are powerful agents of change.

Their voices amplify the message that the fight for freedom is not just about reclaiming land but about reclaiming identity, dignity, and equality. In their defiance and determination, they embody the unbreakable spirit of Palestine.

A Call to the World

The story of Palestinian women is a call to the global community to recognize their struggles and contributions. It is a reminder that gender equality and justice are inseparable from the broader fight for human rights.

By supporting Palestinian women, we support a future where equality and justice prevail, not just in Palestine but everywhere. Their resilience is a beacon of hope, illuminating the path toward a world where freedom and dignity are universal rights.

#20 The Art of Resistance

Cultural Identity Under Siege

Art and culture are powerful tools for resistance, and in Palestine, they serve as a means of preserving identity amidst relentless efforts to erase it. From traditional embroidery and poetry to modern graffiti and music, Palestinian art tells the story of a people who refuse to be silenced.

Under occupation, cultural expression is an act of defiance. The vibrant colors of Palestinian keffiyehs and the intricate patterns of tatreez embroidery are more than just decorative—they are symbols of heritage, resilience, and an unwavering connection to the land.

Graffiti: The Walls Speak

In Palestine, even walls become canvases for expression. Graffiti artists use their skills to transform barriers and checkpoints into spaces of resistance and hope. These murals depict images of freedom, resilience, and the dream of returning to a liberated homeland.

Perhaps the most famous example is the artwork on the separation wall, where local and international artists converge to challenge oppression with powerful imagery and messages. Every stroke of paint is a declaration: "We are here, and we will not be forgotten."

The Power of Poetry

Poetry holds a special place in Palestinian culture. From the verses of Mahmoud Darwish to the improvised rhymes of everyday people, poetry is a means of expressing love for the land, mourning losses, and inspiring hope.

Darwish's words, in particular, have transcended generations, becoming anthems for Palestinians and others who fight for justice. His poetry encapsulates the longing for home, the pain of exile, and the unyielding spirit of resistance.

Music and Dance: A Legacy of Hope

Traditional Palestinian music and dance, such as dabke, are not just forms of entertainment—they are communal acts of resistance. Through these traditions, Palestinians celebrate their culture, defy attempts at erasure, and strengthen their bonds as a community.

Modern Palestinian musicians blend traditional sounds with contemporary influences to create songs that resonate both locally and globally. Artists like Rim Banna and DAM have used their voices to amplify the Palestinian cause, bringing their stories to audiences worldwide.

Theater and Film: Telling the Story

Palestinian theater and film are vital platforms for storytelling, giving voice to the experiences of those living under occupation. Productions like The Freedom Theatre in Jenin and films like Omar and Paradise Now shed light on the complexities of life in Palestine, challenging stereotypes and sparking global conversations.

These art forms humanize the Palestinian struggle, revealing the hopes, fears, and dreams of ordinary people caught in extraordinary circumstances.

A Universal Language of Resistance

Through art, Palestinians communicate their story to the world. Their creations transcend borders and languages, evoking empathy and solidarity from people of all backgrounds. Art becomes a bridge, connecting humanity to the shared values of freedom, justice, and dignity.

Inspiration for the Future

The art of resistance is not just about preserving the past; it is about inspiring the future. Every song, poem, painting, and performance carries the promise of a better tomorrow, where the creativity of a free Palestine can flourish without constraint.

By celebrating and supporting Palestinian art, the global community can ensure that their voices continue to resonate, reminding us all of the enduring power of creativity and resilience.

#21 The Role of International Solidarity

A Global Responsibility

The struggle of Palestine is not just a regional issue; it is a global one. For decades, Palestinians have faced an uphill battle for their basic rights, justice, and dignity. While the majority of the world recognizes the legitimacy of their cause, true change will not come until there is widespread international support for Palestinian self-determination. The role of global solidarity cannot be underestimated.

Solidarity with Palestine goes beyond issuing statements of sympathy. It requires tangible actions that support Palestinian aspirations for peace, justice, and freedom. The international community must stand in solidarity with Palestinians, not only in words but also in deeds that challenge the structures that perpetuate their suffering.

Global Movements for Palestinian Rights

Over the years, global movements have risen in support of Palestinians. The Boycott, Divestment, and Sanctions (BDS) movement, for example, has gained traction as a non-violent method to apply pressure on Israel to end the occupation and grant Palestinians their rights. By calling for boycotts of Israeli goods and divesting from companies that support the occupation, the BDS movement seeks to hold Israel accountable for its actions.

Additionally, grassroots movements across the world—whether in Latin America, Europe, or the United States—have organized protests, campaigns, and advocacy efforts to draw attention to the plight of Palestinians. Through these actions, the international community has shown that the Palestinian cause is not isolated but part of a broader struggle for justice and human rights worldwide.

The Role of Governments

While grassroots movements are vital, the involvement of governments is crucial in securing a lasting solution to the conflict. International diplomatic efforts, such as those spearheaded by the United Nations, the European Union, and other international organizations, have played a role in calling for an end to the occupation and the recognition of Palestine as a state.

However, much more needs to be done. Governments must take stronger stances in holding Israel accountable for violations of international law, including the construction of illegal settlements, the demolition of Palestinian homes, and the systemic violation of Palestinian human rights. The international community must push for a just peace that ensures the rights of both Palestinians and Israelis, based on the principles of equality, freedom, and justice.

Solidarity in Action: Practical Support

International solidarity is not limited to political advocacy—it can take many forms, including humanitarian aid, economic support, and cultural exchange. Organizations around the world provide critical assistance to Palestinians, whether through medical aid, food relief, or rebuilding efforts in Gaza.

Additionally, educational programs and partnerships between Palestinian and international institutions allow for cultural exchange and the sharing of knowledge. These initiatives promote Palestinian voices and bring attention to the rich cultural heritage of the Palestinian people, helping to counter the erasure of Palestinian identity by the occupation.

Supporting Palestinian Voices in Media

One of the most significant ways to show solidarity with Palestine is by amplifying Palestinian voices. The international media plays an important role in shaping global perceptions of the conflict. For too long, Palestinian voices have been marginalized or misrepresented in the media, with narratives often controlled by those with power.

It is vital for international media outlets, filmmakers, journalists, and authors to give Palestinians the platform to share their own stories, experiences, and dreams. Through documentaries, books, articles, and online content, the world can hear firsthand accounts from Palestinians about their struggles, resilience, and hopes for a better future.

The Power of Human Connection

International solidarity is ultimately about human connection. It is about standing up for those who are oppressed, regardless of where they live, and recognizing that their struggle is our own. Solidarity is about standing together, united by a shared commitment to human dignity and justice.

When the world stands with Palestine, it sends a clear message: the struggle for justice does not end at borders. It is a collective endeavor, one that transcends national and ethnic lines, a fight for freedom and dignity for all people.

The Path Forward

For Palestine to truly be free, the global community must continue to work together to advocate for justice, equality, and self-determination for the Palestinian people. This means holding governments accountable, supporting Palestinian civil society, and amplifying the voices of those most affected by the occupation.

The international solidarity movement is not just a phase—it is a commitment to lasting change. It is a commitment to ensuring that future generations of Palestinians grow up in a world where they are free to live, work, and thrive in peace and dignity.

#22 The Spirit of Hope: A Vision for the Future

Palestine's Future: A Dream of Freedom

The road to peace in Palestine is long and fraught with challenges, but the dream of a free and sovereign Palestine endures. The generations that have lived under occupation and exile continue to inspire the world with their resilience and determination to see their homeland restored. Despite the many obstacles, hope remains a powerful force driving the Palestinian people forward.

Palestinians are not just fighting for land; they are fighting for their right to live with dignity, to raise their children in peace, and to determine their own future. The dream of a free Palestine is not just a vision for the Palestinians themselves but a vision for a world in which justice prevails and the rights of all people are respected.

A Vision of Justice and Peace

The solution to the conflict lies in the recognition of justice and the upholding of human rights for all people in the region. This includes the right of Palestinians to return to their homes, the right to self-determination, and the right to live in a state that respects their dignity and sovereignty.

It is crucial that any future solution is based on international law, with an emphasis on the United Nations resolutions that have long called for an end to the occupation and the establishment of a Palestinian state. A peace agreement must recognize the legitimate rights of both Palestinians and Israelis, fostering a future where both peoples can coexist in peace, with mutual respect for their rights and aspirations.

The Role of Palestinian Youth

The future of Palestine lies in the hands of its youth. Palestinian children and young adults have grown up under the shadow of occupation, but they are also the architects of a new era of Palestinian identity and resistance. Today's Palestinian youth are not only educated and motivated but also deeply committed to the cause of freedom and justice.

These young people are redefining what it means to be Palestinian in the 21st century. They are creating innovative solutions to their challenges, leveraging technology, media, and social networks to raise awareness of their plight on the global stage. Through their creativity and determination, they are shaping the future of Palestine, one where their voices are heard and their rights are recognized.

International Advocacy and Diplomacy

For the dream of a free Palestine to become a reality, the international community must remain steadfast in its support. Diplomatic efforts must be directed toward holding Israel accountable for its violations of international law, pushing for meaningful peace negotiations, and advocating for the rights of Palestinians at the United Nations and other international bodies.

However, it is not enough to simply wait for governments to act. Every individual, regardless of nationality, can be an advocate for Palestine. Supporting campaigns, attending protests, educating others, and amplifying Palestinian voices are all powerful ways to contribute to the cause. Solidarity is a powerful force that can bring about change, especially when it is widespread and united in purpose.

The Role of Palestinian Civil Society

Palestinian civil society, despite the challenges it faces, remains a vital force in the quest for justice. Organizations that provide humanitarian aid, promote human rights, and engage in community-building efforts are the backbone of Palestinian society. These organizations have played a critical role in alleviating the suffering of the Palestinian people and helping them maintain a sense of normalcy in the midst of conflict.

Support for Palestinian civil society is essential in ensuring the sustainability of the Palestinian struggle for freedom. By investing in education, healthcare, and economic development, the international community can empower Palestinians to create a future of their own choosing.

A Message of Hope

No matter how difficult the journey, the dream of a free Palestine endures. The resilience of the Palestinian people, the strength of their culture, and the unwavering belief in their right to freedom and justice are the foundation upon which the future of Palestine will be built.

This book serves as a testament to the struggles and sacrifices of the Palestinian people. Yet it also serves as a reminder that the fight for justice is not over. The road may be long, but with hope, solidarity, and a commitment to peace, the dream of a free Palestine can become a reality.

The future is shaped by those who dare to dream. And Palestinians, with the support of the global community, will continue to dream of a future where they are free, where their children can grow up without fear, and where peace and justice prevail for all.

Conclusion: The Unbroken Will of Palestine

A Story of Resilience

The journey of Palestine is not just a narrative of struggle, but also one of immense resilience. For over seventy years, the Palestinian people have endured hardship, loss, and injustice. Yet, despite the many challenges, their spirit remains unbroken. Their steadfastness in the face of adversity is a testament to the strength of the human will and the deep-rooted love for their land, culture, and identity.

Throughout this book, we have witnessed the history, the pain, and the unyielding hope that fuel the Palestinian struggle. We have seen the violence of occupation, the displacement of families, the destruction of homes, and the daily dehumanization of an entire population. But we have also seen the courage, the resistance, and the unwavering belief that Palestine will one day be free.

This story is not just for the people of Palestine; it is for the world. It is a reminder that the struggle for justice is universal, and the fight for freedom cannot be limited by borders or boundaries. The Palestinian cause is a global cause, one that calls upon the conscience of humanity to take action in the face of injustice.

The Strength of Unity

The path to a just and lasting peace in Palestine will require the solidarity of nations, organizations, and individuals. It will require a united front, where people of all backgrounds stand together to demand that Palestinian rights are respected and upheld. The fight for Palestine is not a fight for Palestinians alone; it is a fight for human rights, dignity, and justice for all people.

As the international community continues to rally behind the cause of Palestine, it must remain steadfast in its support. Governments, civil society, and individuals must work together to hold Israel accountable for its violations of international law and ensure that the rights of Palestinians are protected. The fight for Palestine is not a battle of one side versus another; it is a fight for the recognition of humanity, for justice to prevail, and for the healing of a wounded people.

The Promise of Peace

There is a hope that the day will come when Palestinians will live in peace, free from the constant threat of violence and oppression. This hope lies in the belief that the world will one day honor the right of Palestinians to self-determination and allow them to rebuild their lives and their nation. The road to peace will not be easy, but it is a road worth traveling.

Peace in Palestine is not just about the cessation of violence or the end of conflict—it is about justice, reconciliation, and healing. It is about ensuring that the Palestinian people have the freedom to live in dignity, to access basic human rights, and to chart their own future without fear. It is about building a future where Palestinians can finally return to their homes, rebuild their communities, and reclaim the life they were once forced to abandon.

The Call for Action

The struggle of Palestine calls upon the conscience of humanity to act. It is not enough to feel sympathy or express solidarity in words; true solidarity requires action. Whether through political advocacy, humanitarian aid, or public awareness campaigns, every person has the power to contribute to the cause of Palestine. Every small action counts.

To the people of Palestine, the world stands with you. Your struggle is not in vain. Your resilience is an inspiration. And your hope for a better future will continue to inspire generations to come. The journey to freedom is long, but every step you take brings you closer to the day when justice will prevail.

The world must not remain silent in the face of injustice. The Palestinian cause is not a distant, foreign issue—it is a matter of human dignity and equality. It is a call to action that transcends borders and calls upon us all to stand together in the fight for justice and peace.

A Future for Palestine

The future of Palestine is one of possibility. It is a future where children grow up free from the fear of bombs and bullets, where families can live in peace without the constant threat of displacement, and where a nation can thrive, united by the collective will of its people. This future is not just a dream—it is a reality that can be achieved if the world continues to stand in solidarity with Palestine.

The story of Palestine is not one of defeat. It is a story of hope, of strength, and of the unwavering belief that justice will one day prevail. As long as the Palestinian people continue to fight for their rights, as long as the international community continues to advocate for justice, and as long as the spirit of hope remains alive, the dream of a free Palestine will never fade.